WITHDRAWN

ENNIS AND NANCY HAM LIBRARY
ROCHESTER COLLEGE
800 WEST AVON ROAD
ROCHESTER HILLS, MI 48307

17 MINUTES TO LIVE

17 MINUTES TO LIVE

Richard A. Boning

Illustrated by

Harry Schaare

The Incredible Series

Dexter & Westbrook, Ltd., Baldwin, New York

Copyright © 1973 by Dexter & Westbrook, Ltd.

All rights reserved. No part of this book may be reproduced in any form or by any electronic or mechanical means including information storage and retrieval systems without permission in writing from the publisher, except by a reviewer who may quote brief passages in a review. Library of Congress Catalog Card Number: 72-97333

Printed in the United States of America

International Standard Book Number: 0-87966-106-2

To

Gerald Glass

There was not a hint of disaster. It was a bright morning on December 6, 1917. The war in Europe was far away, and people chatted gaily in the streets of Halifax. There was no way of knowing that when the town clock showed five minutes after nine death would come to the city.

Down in the harbor Captain Aime Le Medec was a bundle of nerves. He wiped the perspiration from his brow as his freighter, the French ship *Mont Blanc*, churned through the Narrows leading into Halifax Harbor. It had been a difficult and nerve-racking trip from New York.

"You'll be loaded with explosives," he had been told in New York City. "Hug the shore so the German submarines can't find you."

Aime Le Medec sighed with relief. The journey was almost over. Beside him stood the Canadian pilot, Mackey. In a short time they would be safely at anchor in the harbor. Then there would be time to refuel and plan the long dangerous trip across the Atlantic with munitions for the Allies in Europe.

Suddenly Le Medec noted with curiosity that a ship was approaching from the other end of the channel. It was the *Imo*, a Belgian Relief ship.

"One blast," he ordered. This was the signal for the *Imo* to move over. Dutifully the mate pulled the steam cord, but the *Imo* continued to head directly toward the *Mont Blanc*.

"Fool!" breathed Le Medec. He ordered two blasts to warn the *Imo* to stay on the other side of the channel.

The mate obeyed, but the *Imo* countered with two blasts, indicating she would pass on the starboard side. Le Medec urged the sailor at the helm to bear to port. But it was too late. The prow of the *Imo* ripped into the *Mont Blanc.* The giant ship cut into the smaller freighter like a knife slicing into a loaf of bread. Sparks showered on drums of fuel stored on the forward deck. In a matter of moments the drums burst into flames.

To Le Medec's horror the forward deck became a raging inferno as the *Imo* withdrew from a gaping fifteen-foot wound in the side of the *Mont Blanc.*

To casual bystanders on shore it was one of those things — an unfortunate accident that sometimes happens in crowded ports. None of them suspected the nature of the cargo carried by the French freighter. They could have no way of knowing that now the city of Halifax had only seventeen minutes to live.

Those who noticed the panic of the crew on the *Mont Blanc* could not understand why they were so terrified. But then the harbor was the scene of many strange events. Crews from foreign ports often acted in an unusual manner.

As the heat from the flames seared his face, Le Medec racked his brain. He knew that as soon as the flames reached the explosives, the ship — the crew — and he — Aime Le Medec — would vanish from the face of the earth. There had to be an answer.

The forward deck was already ravaged by fire. It was impossible to reach the hose, which lay burning in the midst of the flames. Then his hopes rose as he thought of the sea valves. He could open them and flood the ship. But that would take a full hour. By then he and his crew would be long in eternity.

There was one last hope. He could run the ship aground. But immediately he realized that this could not possibly prevent the terrible explosion that must come.

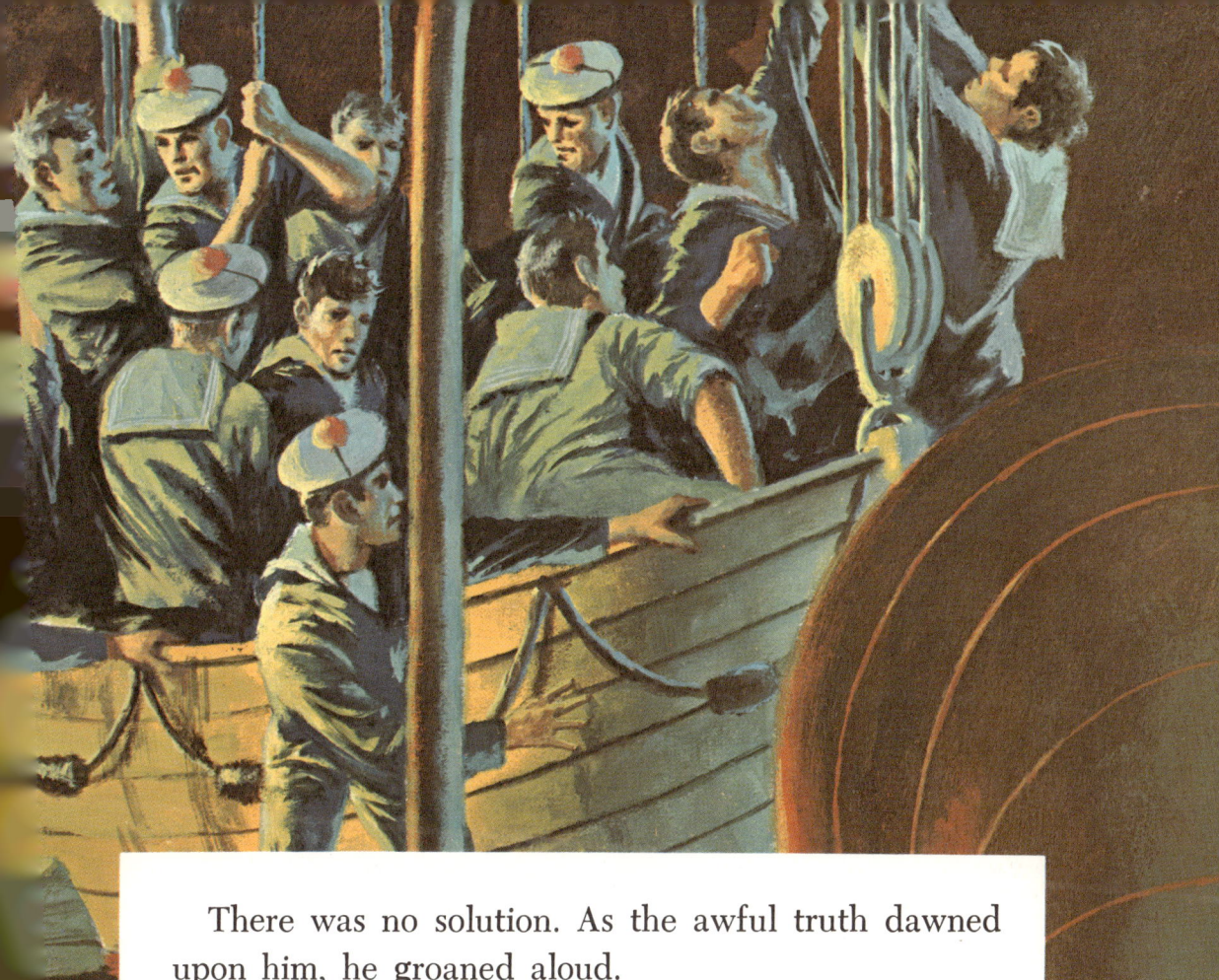

There was no solution. As the awful truth dawned upon him, he groaned aloud.

"Abandon ship!" he commanded.

Then he went below to make certain that all hands had safely left the bowels of the doomed vessel. As the Captain raced through the furnace room, he found that everyone had fled. Returning above deck, he watched his crew prepare to lower the lifeboats. He was overpowered with a feeling of doom. His knees grew weak. As he stared straight ahead with haunted eyes, perspiration glistened on his square black beard. "Lower the boats," he ordered. "Swiftly!" he urged. He had decided to stay aboard and die with his ship.

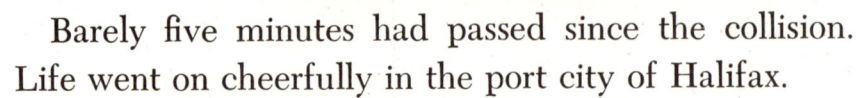

Barely five minutes had passed since the collision. Life went on cheerfully in the port city of Halifax.

On nearby Citadel Hill a boy played with a dog and a red rubber ball. Looking down from above was a teamster. He smiled at the boy as he unloaded boxes from his wagon.

Life was a wonderful thing. The boy had a full measure of it stretching ahead of him. For a moment the teamster felt envious. He glanced at the clock on the City Hall. It read 8:55. He must finish this delivery and return to the warehouse. He did not know it, but time had drawn short indeed. Now the city of Halifax had ten minutes to live.

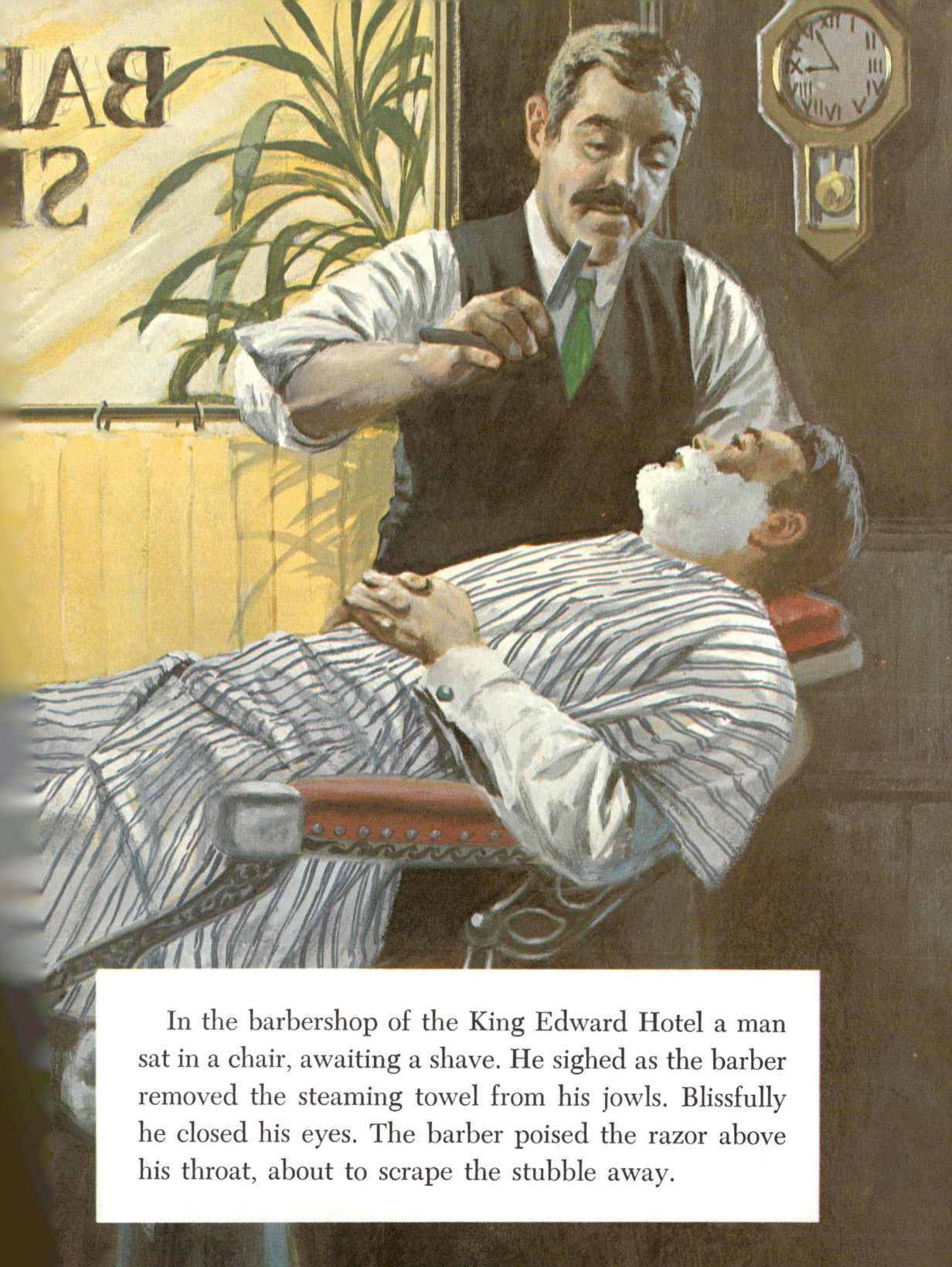

In the barbershop of the King Edward Hotel a man sat in a chair, awaiting a shave. He sighed as the barber removed the steaming towel from his jowls. Blissfully he closed his eyes. The barber poised the razor above his throat, about to scrape the stubble away.

On Pier Number 4 John T. Gammon was startled at the collision in the harbor but not unduly concerned. In a crowded port occasional accidents could not be avoided. His attention soon returned to the task at hand.

Gammon was supervising an underwater project. On the floor of the harbor two divers were building a concrete foundation. As the air pump chugged rhythmically, Gammon returned his gaze to the *Mont Blanc*, now drifting toward Pier Number 6. He noted the bright flames in the forward part of the vessel, and for the first time he felt alarm.

In the West Street Fire Station a telephone rang. Firefighter Billy Wells paid little attention. He stared at the bright engine *Patricia* — the pride and joy of the station. This was the first motor-driven fire engine in Halifax. Billy's fingers itched for the wheel.

A firefighter looked up from the telephone. "A ship's afire off Pier 6!" he said, hanging up the phone. Billy jumped into his boots and donned his slicker. Now he would get a chance to put *Patricia* into action!

In a matter of seconds the shiny red engine was racing over cobblestone streets on its way to the pier a mile and a half away. As he felt the engine respond to the wheel, Billy hoped fervently that he would get there in time to take part in the action. He had no way of knowing he would have to hurry indeed. The city of Halifax had but seven minutes to live.

By now a large group of bystanders watched the French ship with interest. Yells of the excited crew were attracting more attention.

"They're sure mighty upset about something," chuckled an old man.

In the meantime Captain Le Medec closed his eyes, raised his hands to his forehead, and resigned himself to his fate. It would be only a short time now. At that moment his first mate, Jean Glotin, grabbed his shoulder.

"*Mon Capitaine*, we cannot go without you. The boats are waiting. You must come. There is but little time."

Captain Le Medec raised his head and smiled sadly. It was almost too much effort to answer. A great weariness spread through his body. "I know," he said softly, "but a captain must stay with his ship, must he not?"

"*Non, mon Capitaine*," said Glotin. "It would do no good. The crew is waiting in the lifeboats below. We must leave. Now!"

Slowly Le Medec straightened his uniform and began climbing down the ladder to the second lifeboat.

As people on the shore watched with curiosity, the lifeboats left the ship with amazing speed. Both crews leaped to their tasks. Le Medec sat in the stern, wrapped in gloom. Never had onlookers seen rowers pull more furiously.

The flames now glowed more brightly. In a matter of minutes the two boats had reached the wooded shore on the Dartmouth side of the harbor. While citizens watched with amazement, the crew leaped from the boats and ran screaming into the woods.

Now at last the truth became known. "It's loaded with explosives!" cried a horrified bystander. Onlookers shouted a warning to another boat, the *High Flyer*. Members of her crew had rowed over to the *Mont Blanc*, determined to put out the blaze. For a brief moment the crew of the *Mont Blanc*, now safely ashore, watched in disbelief. Le Medec tried to call a final warning as he and his crew fled further into the safety of the forest, their shouts ringing through the woods.

By now the news had spread along the harbor's edge.

"Let's get out of here," said Bill Lovett to telegraph operator Vincent Coleman. "A French munitions ship is going up. If we don't leave, we're finished."

Both men raced for the door. Then suddenly Coleman stopped.

"What about the trains?" he asked. "Two of them are coming this way, loaded with people. They must be stopped."

"Don't be a fool!" his companion said, clutching his sleeve. "You must go. Think of your family."

But Coleman turned back to his telegraph key. Swiftly he rapped out a warning. Never had the key danced more nimbly under his fingers. The message read: "Munitions ship afire, heading for Pier 6. Goodbye."

As the key continued to chatter, his companion turned and raced away.

People along the shore now began to flee in terror. A few of them turned to look at the *Mont Blanc* over their shoulders. At this moment the clock on City Hall said 9:05. For a fraction of a second only — the curious ones witnessed what was to be the last sight of their lives.

A thick orange shaft of light streaked heavenward from the *Mont Blanc*. In the same split second the entire 3,100-ton freighter vanished with a tremendous roar. The crew of the *High Flyer*, who had been battling the flames, disappeared. The force of the explosion was so great that the water was blasted out of the harbor. The 5,000-ton *Imo* was hurled across the channel.

Seagulls high overhead fell in midflight, roasted by the intense heat. A hundred miles away people who had not even heard the explosion noticed that birds flew madly, strangely disturbed. Dishes rattled in cupboards on Prince Edward Island — one hundred and fifty miles away.

As Billy Wells had hoped, he had not arrived too late. Just as *Patricia* screeched around the curve at the foot of Canal Street, Billy heard the tremendous roar. The beautiful new fire engine disappeared. So did his nine companions. As if in a dream, he found himself floating out over the harbor, still clutching the wheel.

A two-ton portion of the *Mont Blanc's* anchor was hurled two miles. Later it would be found on a hillside.

The man sitting in the barber chair in the King Edward Hotel felt a brief sting and then knew no more.

Buildings at the edge of the harbor vanished and with them their inhabitants.

For a square mile the city looked as if it had been pounded into the earth by a giant fist.

As John Gammon, in charge of diving operations on Pier 4, picked himself up, he was greeted with a sight that filled him with horror. The water level of the harbor had dropped ten feet. In a matter of minutes the water would rush back, spreading death and destruction with it.

His first thought was of flight. Suddenly he remembered the divers, still working at the bottom of the harbor. A way must be found to get them up before the tidal wave roared back. The four sailors who had manned the air pump were nowhere to be seen.

"Help!" yelled Gammon to a man nearby. "Give me a hand with this pump."

Without hesitation the stranger set to work pumping life-giving air to the divers below. Gammon tugged frantically on the lines of each diver as he watched the wall of water poised at the entrance of the harbor — ready to sweep back. He prayed the divers would come up in time.

Victims on the surrounding hillside screamed and stared with sightless eyes.

Slowly at first, but then swiftly — tongues of flame began to lick the edges of the buildings. Shrieks from those inside became louder as they smelled the smoke.

Thousands poured from their homes higher up the hill.

"It's a zeppelin attack!" shouted a young girl. "The Germans are bombing us!"

Freak accidents occurred. A sailor was picked up and flung a half mile into the city. Somehow he had survived and found himself stumbling along — all his clothes blown off.

One man who had been out in the harbor found himself and his boat forced to the bottom. He and the boat shot up to the surface again with unbelievable speed.

Miraculously, Billy Wells, the only survivor of his fire crew, stumbled ashore, still clutching the steering wheel of his beloved *Patricia*.

Both trains speeding toward Halifax had been halted in time by the warning of Vincent Coleman. Hundreds of lives had been saved by the brave telegraph operator. Later, all that would be found of him were his brass telegraph key and his watch.

Now the water blown from the harbor began to return in the form of a huge wave, thirty feet high and traveling at the rate of sixty miles an hour.

As he watched, glassy-eyed, Gammon helped the bewildered divers to the surface. He pointed to the mountain of water moving toward them. The divers understood. They lunged frantically for higher ground. As they reached a point of safety, the wall of green water crashed just below them.

The explosion itself continued to roar through the city of Halifax — twisting railroad tracks into the shape of pretzels — flinging buildings about like jackstraws. It swept through the city, carrying a cloud of broken glass from windows.

People screamed in anguish as the small pieces of glass bit into their flesh.

Just as suddenly as it had come, the explosion was over. The city lay in smoking ruins. Thousands were homeless.

On the hill the teamster shook his head in disbelief as he wiped blood from his forehead. He had been struck by a piece of flying glass. He looked around in astonishment to find his horse and wagon gone. Then he gazed down the hill at the spot where seconds before the boy had been playing with a red ball and a dog. All were missing — the ball — the dog — the boy.

Slowly the teamster raised his gaze to the clock on City Hall. The hands had stopped at precisely five minutes past nine. For the boy who had been there just moments ago — and for 2,700 others — death had come to Halifax. Time had stopped forever.

ENNIS AND NANCY HAM LIBRARY
ROCHESTER COLLEGE
800 WEST AVON ROAD
ROCHESTER HILLS, MI 48307